Israel

Marcia S. Gresko

✿ Carolrhoda Books, Inc. / Minneapolis

Photo Acknowledgments

Photos, maps, and artworks are used courtesy of: John Erste, pp. 1, 2–3, 24–25, 37, 41, 43; Laura Westlund, pp. 4, 11; © Alan & Sandy Carey, pp. 6 (both), 8 (both), 11 (bottom), 14 (both), 17 (left), 25 (right), 28, 29 (left), 33; © Richard Lobell Photography, pp. 7 (both), 18 (left), 24, 30 (bottom), 39 (left); © Richard T. Nowitz, pp. 9 (left), 13, 16, 17 (right), 20 (left), 25 (left), 26, 27 (both), 29 (right), 30 (top), 31, 35 (top), 37, 40, 41, 44; © Buddy Mays/TRAVEL STOCK, pp. 9 (right), 22; © James Marshall, pp. 10, 23 (right), 34 (top); © TRIP/A. Tovy, pp. 11 (top), 19, 20 (right), 38, 39 (right); © Jim Simondet, p. 12; © TRIP/S. Shapiro, p. 15 (both); © TRIP/E. James, p. 18 (right); © Nancy Durrell McKenna, p. 21; © TRIP/A. Farago, p. 23 (left); © TRIP/J. Greenberg, p. 32; Maccabiah USA/Sports for Israel, p. 34 (bottom); © Robert Fried, p. 36. Cover photo of Israeli kids by © TRIP/A. Tovy.

Carolrhoda Books, Inc.
A Division of Lerner Publishing Group
241 First Avenue North
Minneapolis, Minnesota 55401 U.S.A.

Website address: www.lernerbooks.com

Words in **bold type** are explained in a glossary that begins on page 44.

Library of Congress Cataloging-in-Publication Data

Gresko, Marcia S.
  Israel / by Marcia S. Gresko
    p. cm. — (A ticket to)
  Includes index.
  Summary: Briefly describes the people, geography, government, religion, language, customs, and lifestyles of Israel.
    ISBN 1-57505-143-5 (lib. bdg. : alk. paper)
    1. Israel—Juvenile literature. [1. Israel.] I. Title
DS118.G877 2000
956.94—dc21   99–41834

Manufactured in the United States of America
1 2 3 4 5 6 – JR – 05 04 03 02 01 00

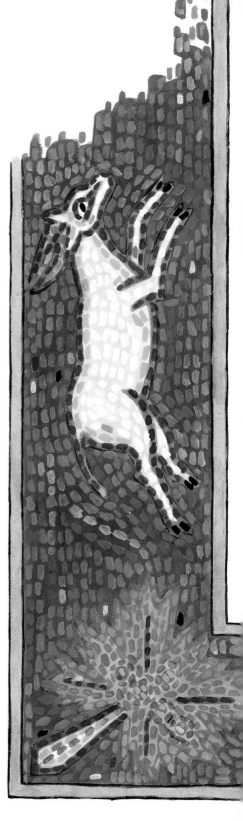

Contents

Welcome!

MEDITERRANEAN SEA

LEBANON

SYRIA

Mt. Meron ▲

Sea of Galilee

Golan Heights

SAMARIAN HILLS

Tel Aviv-Jaffa ●

Jordan River

Gaza Strip

Jerusalem ★

JUDEAN HILLS

Dead Sea

EGYPT

ISRAEL

MIDDLE   EAST

JORDAN

NEGEV DESERT

RED SEA

mountains
highlands
▲ peak
coastal plains
deserts
Great Rift Valley
●●●● disputed border
★ capital city

Miles
0   20   40
0   40   80
Kilometers

N

Gulf of Aqaba

Israel is a country in the **Middle East.** It looks like an arrow pointing south. The warm, blue Mediterranean Sea laps at Israel's western coast. Egypt shares Israel's southwestern border. To the east of Israel sit Syria and Jordan. Israel's northern neighbor is Lebanon. In the south, Israel meets the Gulf of Aqaba, part of the Red Sea.

Map Whiz Quiz

Check out the map on page 4! Use a pencil to trace it onto a piece of paper. Trace the dotted lines, too. People do not agree who should control the land inside the dotted lines.

Find the Mediterranean Sea. Mark it with a "W" for west. Now use a crayon to color it blue. Find the Negev **Desert** and color it brown. Mark the Negev Desert with an "S" for south. Find Lebanon and mark it with an "N" for north.

Green covers the hillsides near the Jordan River (left). The Judean Hills (above) are bare and rocky.

Moving Up

Israel has green fields, brown deserts, and blue waters. The Mediterranean Sea washes the flat coastal **plain.** Look east! You will spot big hills that edge the coastal plains.

Wild Israel

Hundreds of different kinds of birds and butterflies fly over Israel. Gazelles, wild boars, and jackals roam the hills. Foxes and wildcats live in the wooded areas. In the desert, snakes and lizards sun themselves. Ibex *(right)* scramble up rocky cliffs in the mountains.

Past the hills are highlands, which spread over northern and central Israel. Mount Meron is Israel's tallest **mountain.** East of the highlands lies the **Great Rift Valley.**

Jerusalem (below) *rarely gets snow. When it does snow, it melts quickly.*

Heading South

In northeastern Israel's section of the Great Rift Valley, you'll find the sparkling Sea of Galilee. Israel's big river, the Jordan, flows south from the Sea of Galilee. The Jordan

Very little grows in the Negev Desert (above). *The Jordan River* (right) *flows across Israel.*

The Dead Sea is so salty, people can easily float in it (above). *When the water dries up, strange salt sculptures stay behind* (left).

winds through the Great Rift Valley to the Dead Sea—the lowest spot on the earth's surface. The water in the Dead Sea is so salty that fish can't live there.

Farther south you will find the bare Negev Desert. This hot, rocky desert covers the southern half of Israel.

More than 425,000 people call Jerusalem home.

Golden Jerusalem

Jerusalem, the **capital** of Israel, sits on a hilltop in the highlands. People used pale yellow stone to build most of the city, so Jerusalem can look as if it were made of gold.

A visit to Jerusalem is like traveling to two cities at once! The western half looks modern. In the older, eastern part of the

city, folks shop at lively open-air markets or visit ancient buildings. Some buildings are a thousand years old!

In Jerusalem's Old City, visitors will find ancient structures (top) and bustling markets called souks (right).

History Lesson

Israel was an ancient Jewish kingdom. Then conquering rulers sent away the Jewish people, who made new homes all over the world. Centuries later **ethnic Arabs** settled in Israel, then known as Palestine.

Israel's flag is blue and white like a Jewish prayer shawl. The six-pointed Star of David, a traditional Jewish symbol, fills the center.

In 1948 Jewish people founded the modern nation of Israel. Millions of Jews joyfully returned to their ancient homeland. After a war, many Palestinians left. Other Palestinians want to control part of Israel, where their people have lived for over a thousand years. These days Arab and Jewish Israelis (people who live in Israel) do not always get along.

The Holocaust

The Holocaust was the murder of six million European Jews by Nazis during World War II (1939–1945). Nazis forced the Jews into **concentration camps** and killed them. After the war, many of the survivors moved to Israel. Monuments and museums help Israelis remember the Holocaust and honor the people who died, as well as those who survived.

Yad Va'Shem Museum in Jerusalem

Different Faces

Four out of five Israelis are Jews. But their families might have come from North or South America, Asia, Europe, or Africa. Because Israelis have ancestors from all

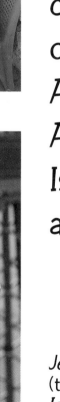

Jewish kids share a picnic lunch (top). Schoolgirls from northern Israel take a stroll (left).

over the world, the Jewish people of Israel do not all look, talk, or dress alike. They eat different

Jewish Israeli kids from Russia

foods, listen to different music, and tell different **folktales.** These people work together to make Israel a good place to live.

Make Yourself at Home!

People who move to Israel might speak French, German, Polish, Hungarian, Ethiopian, or Russian! The Israeli government has set up free centers where newcomers can learn the Hebrew language and the customs of their new home.

The Arabs

About a million ethnic Arabs live in Israel. Arabs have lived in the area since the middle of the A.D. 600s. Most Israeli Arabs are Muslims, which means that they follow the religion Islam. In years past, most Arabs lived on small farms. These days more Arabs live in cities.

Muslims choose from different styles of dress.

Many grown-ups work in shops or are builders on construction sites. Israeli Arabs usually speak Arabic.

Nomads

Some of Israel's Arabs are Bedouin. The Bedouin are known as the "Lords of the Desert." Some Bedouin are **nomads** who pitch tents wherever they find grass for their herds of goats. But many Bedouin have settled in desert towns, where they farm and send their children to school.

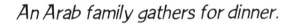

An Arab family gathers for dinner.

A family takes an afternoon stroll (left). Meals are special times for family members to gather (above).

City Life

Most Israelis live in high-rise apartment buildings in cities. Many apartments have balconies where families can relax on hot nights. Kids spend most days at school.

Moms and dads might work in stores, factories, or offices.

Israelis in the city can spend their time off at museums, stores, and restaurants. Some drive to the beach or to a park.

All in the Family

Here are the Hebrew words for family members. Practice using these terms on your own family.

father	*abba*	(AH-bah)
mother	*eema*	(EE-mah)
uncle	*dod*	(DOHD)
aunt	*dodda*	(DOH-dah)
grandfather	*sabba*	(SAH-bah)
grandmother	*savta*	(SAHV-tah)
son	*ben*	(BEHN)
daughter	*bat*	(BAHT)
brother	*ach*	(ACH)
sister	*achot*	(ah-CHOT)

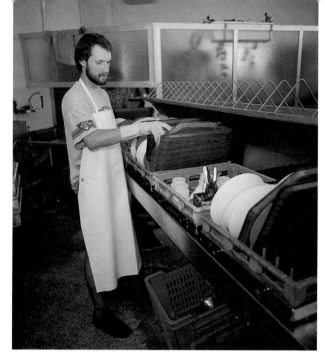

Kibbutzniks (people who live and work on a kibbutz) eat together (left). Washing dishes (above) is one of the many chores on a kibbutz.

On a Kibbutz

Some Israeli kids live on a **kibbutz,** a settlement in the countryside. Each kibbutz is like a village, with houses, shops, and a school. Farm fields usually spread nearby, and there might be a factory. People on a

The Children's House

Meet Tal! He is 10 years old and lives on Kibbutz Erez. Kids who live on a kibbutz might spend time at a Children's House. Kids learn, play, and hang out together at the Children's House. Most kids are assigned to a group with children the same age.

kibbutz eat meals and celebrate holidays together.

Everyone works hard to make the kibbutz run. People take turns doing different jobs. After spending a few weeks washing dishes, a worker might pick fruit.

Religion

Jewish people practice Judaism, the oldest major religion in the world. Jews believe in one God. The Torah (the first five books of the Bible) contains the history of the Jewish people and the basic laws of Judaism. The laws tell Jews how to live a good life and how to pray.

Some Israeli Jews are Orthodox. They follow traditional customs, such as how to dress and what to eat or drink. They pray many times a day.

(Above) *Every Friday Muslims gather at a mosque—the Muslim place of worship. The Koran* (inset) *is the Islamic holy book.*

The prophet Muhammad founded the religion Islam. Muslims believe in one God, called Allah, who shared wisdom with the prophet Muhammad. This knowledge is recorded in a sacred book called the Koran.

Hebrew letters (above)
spell out "shalom."
A child practices
writing in Hebrew (left).

Two Languages

Shalom! That means "peace" in Hebrew.
Israelis use the word to say both "hello" and
"good-bye." Arabic speakers say "salaam."
Hebrew and Arabic are Israel's two official
languages. Both languages are written from
right to left—that's the opposite direction of

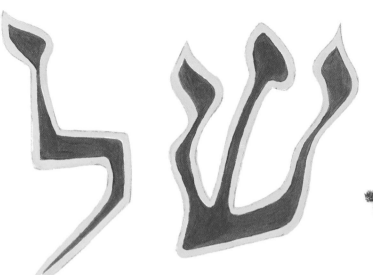

written English. Hebrew and Arabic each have their own alphabet.

Books in Israel are commonly printed in Hebrew.

Eliezer Ben-Yehuda

In modern times, more than 60 percent of Israelis speak Hebrew regularly. But for 2,000 years, the Hebrew language was only spoken in prayers. Jewish people spoke many different languages in countries around the world. In 1881 Eliezer Ben-Yehuda immigrated to Israel (then Palestine). He worked to make Hebrew the language spoken in everyday life.

Money, stamps, and street signs (above) *are printed in Hebrew, Arabic, and English.*

Celebrate!

In the fall, Jewish Israelis celebrate Rosh Hashana, the Jewish new year. Jews say prayers and have a special dinner. Yom Kippur also comes in the fall. Yom Kippur is a time for Jews to fast (not eat or drink) and to think about how to live a good life.

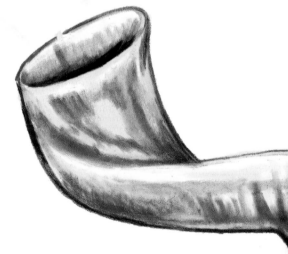

A blast from the shofar (a ram's-horn trumpet) signals the start of Rosh Hashana.

Muslims show their faith during the month of Ramadan. They fast from sunrise to sunset. The month ends with a three-day party.

Israelis in Jerusalem celebrate Israel's Independence Day.

Purim!

Purim, a Jewish holiday, is like Halloween and April Fool's Day in one! Newspapers run made-up stories. People throw costume parties and watch colorful parades. Even the **synagogue** is noisy!

School Days

School is out! Teachers and students head home after a school day.

Kids in Israel go to school six days a week. Jewish kids get Saturdays off, and Muslim kids have Fridays off. Those are the holy days in their religions.

In Israel most children of different religions go to separate schools. Jewish kids learn math, science, language arts, and social studies. The classes are taught in Hebrew.

They also study the Torah and Jewish history.

Muslim students take most of the same classes as Jewish kids, but the lessons are in Arabic. Muslim students learn about Islam and the history of Arab people instead of about Judaism.

Muslim kids head to school.

Plant a Tree!

Tu B'Shevat is Israel's holiday for planting trees. Over the years, schoolchildren have planted more than two hundred million trees.

Growing Up

Jewish boys and girls can become official adults in the Jewish community at age 13. A boy becomes a bar mitzvah. A girl becomes a bat mitzvah. The words mean "son (or

In a ceremony to become a bar mitzvah, a boy chants from the Torah (top). Jewish kids attend religious school (left).

Men and women in the Israeli Defense Force play tug-of-war.

daughter) of the Commandments." After a ceremony, families usually have a special celebration.

At age 18, Israeli teenagers serve in the Israeli Defense Force (army). Men serve for three years. Unmarried women serve for 21 months.

A vendor in the Old City sells steaming plates of food.

Snack Break

When you get hungry in Israel, you can choose between many different foods. Street vendors offer tasty falafel—mashed, fried chickpeas (garbanzo beans)—wedged into a pita (pocket bread). Sellers top it with salad and a tasty sauce. Some diners stop for a burger and fries. Others grab fresh, delicious fruit for a healthy snack. Israelis believe that they grow the world's best fruit. Try an orange or a date!

At the Market

Although Israelis can buy their food at the supermarket, most shop at small corner grocery stores or **bargain** at busy open-air markets called souks. The sellers and buyers spend time trying to agree on a price. Shoppers find stalls piled high with fruits and vegetables, pots, pans, blue jeans, and comic books!

Soccer anyone?

A runner takes her mark at the Maccabiah Games.

Time to Play!

Many Israelis like to play sports—especially soccer! Kids play in schoolyards or join youth leagues. Fans pack the stadiums to cheer for their favorite professional team.

Dig It!

Many Israelis are interested in the country's far-off past. Experts study ancient ruins to learn more about Israel's history. They dig into hillsides to find the ruins of ancient cities.

Israel hosts its own Olympic-style games every four years. The Maccabiah Games bring together Jewish athletes from around the world. Events include basketball, volleyball, track and field, tennis, boxing, water sports, gymnastics, fencing, wrestling, and table tennis.

Many years ago, artists decorated Dome of the Rock with colorful patterns.

Art Everywhere

It is easy to find art in Israel. Beautiful
stained glass windows reflect light in the
synagogue at the Hadassah Hospital in
Jerusalem. Colorful mosaics (pictures made
from placing pieces of colored glass, stone,

or tile into cement) decorate the mosque Dome of the Rock. At shops in the Old City, sellers display fine embroidery, gleaming brass work, and elegant carvings. Browsers can admire beautiful jewelry at the stalls.

A colorful mosaic fish

A beautiful stained glass window

Israelis gather in local parks for Saturday dances (left). *Local musicians take their beat on the street* (facing page top).

Tunes and Twirls

Israelis gather to sing at their neighbors' homes, in kibbutz cafeterias, and around campfires. Modern vocal music borrows from folk songs, patriotic songs, poetry, and rock and roll. Most cities and towns boast an orchestra. Listeners enjoy klezmer music's foot-stomping rhythm and wailing clarinet.

Dancing is a fun way to spend a Saturday night! Many Israelis like energetic Arab line dances and whirling Romanian circle dances.

Glittering Tel Aviv-Jaffa

Tel Aviv-Jaffa is Israel's second largest city. Lively theater groups, fine museums, and interesting art galleries dot the city. The world-famous Israel Philharmonic Orchestra makes its home in Tel Aviv-Jaffa.

Good Book!

These book lovers shop for their favorite stories during Hebrew Book Week.

Looking for something to read? You won't have to go far. Most city streets have newsstands packed with newspapers and magazines. Bookstores are jammed with books on all sorts of subjects in many different languages.

Newsstands in Israel are stocked with newspapers in many different languages.

Each year during Hebrew Book Week, cities and towns turn their plazas and parks into large, open-air bookstores. Israelis find enough bargains to fill their bookshelves!

Folktales

Israeli kids love to hear the folktales that their relatives brought with them from all over the world. Here is a story told by Jewish people with an Eastern European heritage.

A man lived with his wife and many children in a tiny, busy, crowded house. The man wanted some peace and quiet, so he asked a rabbi what to do. The rabbi said, "Bring your chickens into your house."

The man was surprised, but he did what the rabbi advised. The chickens made the noise and crowding worse! When the man went back for more advice, the rabbi told him to bring a different animal inside every day. The man brought in goats, ducks, and a cow. Fur, feathers, people, and noise filled the house.

After a week, the rabbi advised the man to take the honking, clucking, mooing animals outside. That night the man and his family slept in peace. The next morning, the man looked around his tiny house and said, "What a peaceful place!"

43

New Words to Learn

bargain: A talk between a buyer and seller about the cost of an item. Bargaining ends when both sides agree on a price.

capital: A city where the government is located.

concentration camp: A prison camp that confines people believed by the group running the government to be dangerous.

desert: A dry, sandy region that receives low amounts of rainfall.

ethnic Arabs: Modern-day relatives of the people who settled Israel in the A.D. 600s.

Vendors in Jerusalem offer fresh bagels.

folktale: A timeless story told by word of mouth from grandparent to parent to child. Many folktales have been written down in books.

Great Rift Valley: A low area of the earth's surface that stretches all the way from Syria to Mozambique. The Red Sea is part of the Great Rift Valley.

kibbutz: An Israeli farming settlement where people share work and belongings.

Middle East: A part of southwestern Asia that meets North Africa. Countries in the Middle East include Israel, Jordan, Syria, Iran, Iraq, and Egypt.

mountain: A part of the earth's surface that rises high into the sky.

nomad: A person who moves from place to place, following seasonal sources of water and food.

plain: A broad, flat area of land that has few trees or other outstanding natural features.

stained glass: Colored glass arranged to make a picture.

synagogue: A Jewish house of worship.

New Words to Say

bar mitzvah	BAHR MITS-vah
bat mitzvah	BAHT MITS-vah
Bedouin	BEH-doh-ihn
falafel	fah-LAH-fehl
Galilee	GA-lih-lee
Islam	ihs-LAHM
Israel	IHZ-ree-ehl
Israeli	ihz-RAY-lee
kibbutz	kih-BUHTS
Muslim	MOOS-lihm
Negev	NEH-gehv
Palestine	PA-leh-styn
Ramadan	RAH-mah-dahn
salaam	sah-LAHM
shalom	shah-LOHM
shofar	SHOH-fahr
synagogue	SIH-nuh-gahg
Yom Kippur	YOHM kih-POOR

More Books to Read

Allard, Denise. *Postcards from Israel.* Austin, TX: Raintree Steck-Vaughn, 1997.

Bacon, Josephine. *Cooking the Israeli Way.* Minneapolis: Lerner Publications Company, 1986.

Cahill, Jane. *Israel.* Philadelphia: Chelsea House Publishers, 1999.

Ganeri, Anita. *I Remember Palestine.* Austin, TX: Raintree Steck-Vaughn, 1995.

Israel in Pictures. Minneapolis: Lerner Publications Company, 1989.

Taylor, Allegra. *A Kibbutz in Israel.* Minneapolis: Lerner Publications Company, 1987.

Waldman, Neil. *Masada.* New York: Morrow Junior Books, 1998.

New Words to Find